At Issue

| Racial Profiling

Other Books in the At Issue Series:

At Issue

Racial Profiling

Kathy L. Hahn, Book Editor

GREENHAVEN PRESS
A part of Gale, Cengage Learning

Detroit • New York • San Francisco • New Haven, Conn • Waterville, Maine • London

GALE
CENGAGE Learning™

Christine Nasso, *Publisher*
Elizabeth Des Chenes, *Managing Editor*

© 2011 Greenhaven Press, a part of Gale, Cengage Learning.

Gale and Greenhaven Press are registered trademarks used herein under license.

For more information, contact:
Greenhaven Press
27500 Drake Rd.
Farmington Hills, MI 48331-3535
Or you can visit our Internet site at gale.cengage.com

For product information and technology assistance, contact us at

Gale Customer Support, 1-800-877-4253
For permission to use material from this text or product, submit all requests online at www.cengage.com/permissions

Further permissions questions can be e-mailed to permissionrequest@cengage.com

Articles in Greenhaven Press anthologies are often edited for length to meet page requirements. In addition, original titles of these works are changed to clearly present the main thesis and to explicitly indicate the author's opinion. Every effort is made to ensure that Greenhaven Press accurately reflects the original intent of the authors. Every effort has been made to trace the owners of copyrighted material.

LIBRARY OF CONGRESS CATALOGING-IN-PUBLICATION DATA

Racial Profiling / Kathy L. Hahn, book editor.
    p. cm. -- (At issue)
    Includes bibliographical references and index.
    ISBN 978-0-7377-5093-5 (hardcover) -- ISBN 978-0-7377-5094-2 (pbk.)
    1. Racial profiling in law enforcement--Juvenile literature. I. Hahn, Kathy L.
    HV7936.R3R326 2010
    363.2'32--dc22
    2010015895

Printed in the United States of America
1 2 3 4 5 6 7 14 13 12 11 10

Contents

Introduction

On January 12, 2010, a young musician, Jordan Miles, was confronted by Pittsburgh plainclothes police. Photos taken by Jordan's mother reveal the result of that confrontation—a bruised face, swollen cheek and lip, and right eye swollen shut. There was also a bald spot in her son's scalp where the 18-year-old violinist says police tore dreadlocks from his head after stopping and arresting him. The reason police gave for stopping Jordan was that they suspected he had a gun under his coat, which proved to be a soda bottle. Although the three white officers who arrested him have been reassigned, Jordan's mother, Terez Miles, believes justice has not been served: "I feel that my son was racially profiled. . . . It's a rough neighborhood; it was after dark . . . (the police) assumed he was up to no good because he's black. My son, he knows nothing about the streets at all. He's had a very sheltered life, he's very quiet, he doesn't know police officers sit in cars and stalk people like that."[1]

A more notorious, but perhaps less cut-and-dry, incident is that of a 58-year-old Harvard University professor who was "caught" trying to break into his own home in Cambridge, Massachusetts. On the afternoon of July 16, 2009, Henry Louis Gates Jr. was arrested. Much was made of the fact that the original 911 caller, a concerned neighbor, reported to the dispatcher that "two black males" were attempting to jimmy the front door across the way.[2] Many argue that the arresting officer, a Cambridge police sergeant, known for his efforts to encourage good race relations in his department and in the community, was simply doing his job by stopping the "break-in" in progress and detaining Gates, an African-American, un-

---

1. Information courtesy of *newsone*, http://newsone.com/nation/associated-press/teen-violinist-says-police-beat-him-and-tore-off-dreadlock/, January 22, 2010.
2. Information courtesy of *huffingtonpost.com*, http://www.huffingtonpost.com/2009/07/20/henry-louis-gates-jr-arre_n_241407.html, July 20, 2009.

til the matter could be sorted out. Others, however, contend that the officer's reaction was racially motivated. For whatever reason, Gates ended up being arrested, and charges of racial profiling and harassment immediately were heard across the country. Not surprisingly, both men's stories reflect differing views of what actually happened. A case such as this defines the issue in succinct clarity: Where does good, solid police work begin, and where should it end, when law enforcement interacts with members of a minority group?

In truth, only an apprehending officer can know whether he or she is motivated to detain someone based on professional knowledge and experience, or on an underlying agenda of discrimination or bias. Law enforcement agencies, whose responsibilities are growing and becoming more complex, find themselves walking a precarious line between justifiable detainment and racially motivated behavior. Although individual officers always bring their own subjectivity and discretion to each situation, sensitivity training and the reinforcement of regulated standards are the keys to reducing discrimination and profiling.

It is clear, however, that the easing or elimination of racial profiling cannot be accomplished solely by efforts made on the part of law enforcement; citizens also must contribute by allowing police to do their job and by giving police the benefit of the doubt that not every action committed by an officer against someone of minority status is a sign of profiling. As society continues to merge and diverge, the potential for profiling and accusations of profiling also will increase. The authors of the following viewpoints in *At Issue: Racial Profiling* examine the issue from a variety of perspectives.

1

Racial Profiling Helps to Prevent Crimes

Chris E. McGoey

Chris E. McGoey is a security expert and consultant specializing in security management, crime, and loss prevention.

To prevent loss from theft, retail store owners and security personnel must remain vigilant toward people who fit the profile of a shoplifter. At the same time, owners and officers also must guard against the tendency toward profiling shoplifters solely on race, rather than on other key "warning signals" of persons typically prone to the crime. For example, regardless of race or ethnicity, an individual standing alone with a large empty shopping bag could be a potential thief intending to steal; to this extent, profiling is a valuable tool and should not be discouraged.

The media often asks me if retail store security personnel use "profiling" tactics as a means of determining which customers are most likely to steal. The answer is undeniably, yes.

Profiling Is a Tool

The concept of shoplifter profiling is a proven loss-prevention tool and is currently being practiced in most major retail stores by trained loss prevention or security staff. Does that seem shocking? It shouldn't, as long as it doesn't include the discriminatory practice of focusing on the race of the customer alone. Profiling is used every day as a method for quickly focusing in on a person, a product line or a section of a store most likely to contribute to shoplifting. All investigative agencies including the police, FBI [Federal Bureau of Investigation], and others have used profiling as a tool to narrow the field of possible suspects. Why shouldn't retail store security be able to do the same? Store and customer profiles are developed during day-to-day operation and by collecting and analyzing inventory data. These data provide both a quantitative and a qualitative basis for determining where, when, how, and by whom shoplifting is likely to occur in the future.

Profiling like this makes perfect business sense because it is legal and a good business practice.

A progressive retailer has numerous inventory controls in effect and at several levels. Every store should know what departments and which product lines have the greatest inventory loss based on audits, product movement analysis reports, shoplifter apprehensions, and by finding signs of theft. Professional retail loss prevention personnel are trained to know what day of the week, what time of day, what product lines, and what department will have the most shoplifting activity. Armed with these data, loss prevention personnel set out to observe shopper "conduct" in the most active areas and during the most active times. Profiling like this makes perfect business sense because it is legal and a good business practice.

There are other types of profiling based on store apprehension histories and industry experience that has taught LP [loss prevention] professionals who to "include" and who to "exclude" when scanning the store for potential shoplifters. For example, one profile is that people rarely shoplift while in the presence of their spouse, significant other, or parents. After scanning these persons they might quickly be bypassed as theft candidates. Shoplifting is a crime of opportunity and desire. Trained loss prevention staff will spend most of their time observing those customers whose conduct demonstrates both opportunity and desire. For example, a customer standing alone in a remote aisle, carrying a large empty shopping bag, and looking from side-to-side would be immediately suspicious until their conduct proves otherwise.

If trained professionals do the surveillance properly, most people will never realize they were observed while shopping.

A customer wearing tattered shoes might appear suspicious in a self-service shoe department until their conduct disproved a lack of desire to steal. A customer walking across a store carrying a small electronic item partially concealed in the palm of their hand might seem suspicious until several opportunities passed to conceal the product. In contrast, a customer wearing tailored shorts and a t-shirt may have the desire to steal, but will have little opportunity to conceal a large item of merchandise they are carrying. Based on profiling and shopper conduct, the professional plain-clothes security officer will scan thousands of customers a day and determine that 99% of them are legitimate shoppers.

Surveillance Is Necessary

Believe me, merchants don't like monitoring their customers to prevent theft, but they know that it's a matter of economic survival. Merchants know that closely watching customers is bad public relations if done crudely. However, the retail industry loses over 31.3 billion dollars every year and shoplifting represents about one-third of it. Customer surveillance is limited to the public areas where there is no expectation of privacy as opposed to inside fitting rooms and restrooms that are considered private areas. Knowing that you are under surveillance is an uneasy feeling. No one likes being watched and being made to feel like you're not trustworthy. However, if trained professionals do the surveillance properly, most people will never realize they were observed while shopping. A problem can arise when untrained or unqualified security, loss prevention or off-duty police undertake the task of store surveillance. The majority of the complaints of racial profiling that I have seen in retail stores have to do with the perception of being stalked throughout the store in an effort to intimidate them into leaving.

Racial Profiling

Racial profiling is an improper and illegal practice based on the mistaken belief that certain ethnic groups are more likely to shoplift than others. Because of this, misguided store employees will focus their surveillance time on the customer's "color" rather than "conduct". Racial bias can blind store personnel and cause them to monitor only the ethic minorities and ignore the real source of their inventory losses. Racial profiling eventually leads to a pattern of false theft accusations, wrongful detentions, and harassment when no real probable cause exists. The result is that a particular ethic group will be made to feel like they can't be trusted and are unwelcome in the store. African Americans call it "shopping while black". Unless the wrongful conduct is corrected by management, civil rights violations will occur and false arrest lawsuits will follow and sorely damage the reputation of the retailer.

Off-duty police officers working as security need training too.

Customer surveillance based solely on the race of a customer is not only improper but is an ineffective method of controlling losses due to shoplifting. The thought of racial profiling is distasteful. A 1999 Gallup poll confirmed that 81% of Americans disapprove of the practice. Despite this belief, the same poll indicated that 75% of African American men said they had been victims of racial profiling while shopping.

Most major retailers have published policies against discriminatory acts but few that I've seen specifically address racial profiling by its security personnel. Not surprisingly, incidents are occurring, which feeds the question of how much racial profiling exists in retail stores? For example, in one major department store the security staff used radio codes (code 3) as an alert anytime a black shopper came into the area. In another store, 90% of the shoplifting apprehensions were of ethnic customers where the store demographic reports only showed a 15% minority customer base. And in still another store, sales associates were told by security officers to call them anytime an ethnic minority entered their sales area.

Hiring, Training, and Supervision

The only way to eliminate racial profiling is to prohibit it from the top. Retail stores need to have clearly defined and articulated policies against security staffers practicing racial profiling and must have a zero tolerance for abuse. The hiring process is a good time to screen out poor candidates that seem predisposed to prejudice. Comprehensive retail security training is absolutely necessary to ensure that employees know how to do the job appropriately and understand the rules of conduct. Off-duty police officers working as security need training too. You can't assume that they understand the law or will act appropriately and fairly toward all customers especially in the retail setting. Off-duty police officers must follow store rules when on the clock and not resort to street tactics when dealing with store customers. During the training phase new loss prevention personnel should be taught how to observe customer conduct and not base surveillance decisions solely on the race of the customer. Supervisors should always be on the lookout for signs of racial prejudice in day-to-day conversation and in written reports. Violations should be addressed swiftly. If racial profiling becomes a factor in security staff surveillance and detentions, it's because store management didn't care enough to correct the problem or instead chose to ratify the behavior.

2

Accusations of Racial Profiling Are Counterproductive

Sidhartha Banerjee and Brenda Branswell

Sidhartha Banerjee and Brenda Branswell have written for The Gazette *(Montreal).*

Police are trained to be suspicious, but in an ever-increasing world of sensitivity toward racial profiling, their duties often are difficult to perform without seeming to be based upon some underlying bias or prejudice. True incidents of profiling on the part of law enforcement combine with false accusations on the part of community members to create a continual state of mutual distrust.

Brian Copeland was having a good time sightseeing in Montreal last July [2004]—until, he said, police stopped him on Ste. Catherine St. and asked for identification.

"The first thing they said was 'you look like someone we're looking for,'" said Copeland, a 6-foot-6 science teacher from Brooklyn, N.Y., who suggested he doesn't resemble many people.

"I think the whole thing was fake—'you look like someone.'"

Copeland, who is black, doesn't believe they were looking for anybody. In fact, he insisted their explanation was a classic line used in racial profiling.

The police, however, offered a different perspective in a letter Copeland shared with *The Gazette*. In response to a missive Copeland sent to Montreal Mayor Gerald Tremblay, police Lt. Stephane Belanger noted "being stopped by a police officer alone does not constitute racial profiling."

Natural Suspicion, or Racist Attitudes?

Racial profiling—singling out citizens for stereotypical, prejudicial or racist reasons rather than reasonable suspicion—is a sensitive issue that irks police forces accused of it.

"So much of police work is playing odds."

It can also be a murky one since police, by the very nature of their work, look for suspects.

"And there's the rub, you see, because police have to profile. . . . But they have to have evidentiary reasons," said Myrna Lashley, a psychologist who teaches at John Abbott College [in Montreal].

"You can't just go up to somebody and say because your skin colour is yellow or your skin is black, you're automatically a suspect. That's where racial profiling comes in," said Lashley, who is vice-chairperson of the board at L'Ecole Nationale de Police du Quebec [The National Police School of Quebec] in Nicolet.

"So much of police work is playing odds," added Jim Anderson, head of John Abbott College's police technology program.

"But there is a fine line between using your police judgment and developing racist attitudes that if someone is wearing a fancy suit or acting in a certain manner or driving a certain kind of car, they're immediately a suspect."

Montreal Police Single Out Black Drivers

Yet many black Montrealers clearly believe some officers—not all—cross that line.

They recounted their experiences to *The Gazette* about being stopped or followed by police on the road but not given a ticket—scrutiny they felt was prompted by their skin colour.

Skepticism arises among blacks about police explanations for a stop because they have heard them so often.

"You hear about these things all the time," said Michael Gittens, director of the Cote des Neiges Black Community Association. People say they were stopped and asked questions about who the vehicle belongs to, he said.

It isn't only young black males. Lashley said she was pulled over last year on Nun's Island [Quebec], but insisted she hadn't committed an infraction. The officer didn't ask for her license, only her name, she said.

"I thought, ah man, this is a DWB," Lashley said, referring to the term "driving while black."

"I said to him in my strongest tone, I am Doctor Myrna Lashley." The officer said "Oh, OK" and left, she said.

Lashley noted she has also had positive experiences with police. She suggested it would be helpful if they provided people with more information about why they are being stopped. Skepticism arises among blacks about police explanations for a stop because they have heard them so often, she said. So people don't believe it "even if it is true."

"What happens is now you've got double perception: who's right, who's wrong?"

Police Department Demands Accountability from Its Officers

Montreal police officially banned racial profiling last year by making it against departmental policy.

Deputy police chief Yves Charette said this week he doesn't believe racial profiling is a widespread practice among the force.

Still, in mid-March, Charette said police plan to hold a teaching session with their most senior staff to look at how to better educate the force's officers.

"We want to make sure we're on the same wavelength—that the message (is) that racial profiling is against policy," said assistant police chief Jacques Lelievre, who is in charge of the police force's attempt to combat racial profiling.

As for random stops, Lelievre said: "I wouldn't be happy to be stopped, but it's normal and it happens, whether its a random stop or a roadblock. It's never fun."

A police officer can randomly pull someone over to verify their license and registration, if they suspect someone has been driving drunk, or if there is something mechanically wrong with the car, he said. "It has to be absolutely random if there is nothing apparent," Lelievre said. "Any other reasons are unacceptable."

Each time someone is stopped, police log it on their on-board vehicle computer, detailing license plate and location. "But it doesn't provide enough immediate information to allow commanding officers to know exactly what happened," Lelievre said.

Statistical Data Compilation May Help Track Incidents of Profiling

Which is one reason some observers call for race-based data collection—a practice conducted in Kingston, Ont.—so that police stops can be tracked.

"One of the possible benefits of collecting data is that it provides transparency," said Scot Wortley, a professor with the Centre of Criminology at the University of Toronto.

"The idea is there are allegations of racial profiling and you need to be transparent with what you do—one way is by collecting these data and showing you have nothing to hide."

Wortley, an expert on race, crime and policing and a proponent of data tracking, said Canadian police are falling behind counterparts in Britain and the United States, where tracking has been in place for nearly 15 years.

The Quebec Human Rights Commission is handling between 20 and 25 cases involving racial profiling allegations.

"Each time something appears in the media, it destroys the trust we build daily."

Researchers and experts say the perception is very real and that alone is enough to study racial profiling further. "It's irrefutable right now. There have been enough surveys done, public opinion surveys and commissions that document that the black community in Ontario and Quebec perceive the justice system is biased against them," Wortley said. "You can no longer say that it's just a few radical people in the community (who) are making such allegations."

Police and Community Members Must Learn to Trust Each Other

Following a series of stories on race and crime in 2002 by the *Toronto Star* recommendations were made by the Ontario Human Rights Commission on how to improve policing practices. In December, one year after the report was published, little progress had been seen on any front in Toronto.

In Montreal, the police force has taken measures to fight discriminatory practices, offering training for rookie and veteran officers who may be considered intolerant.

Police brass feel they've come a long way toward building a climate of trust with cultural communities.

Yet Montreal police brotherhood boss Georges Painchaud said morale dips among the 4,200 members each time a negative story about police and race hits the media. "There are isolated cases, but the accusations are levelled at the entire force," said Painchaud, who says the police union has a firm policy against racism.

"It's always 'the police,' and that's very frustrating for the officers."

"The officers work hard at community policing—particularly in ethnic and black communities," he said. "But each time something appears in the media, it destroys the trust we build daily."

Perhaps compounding the issue is the mistrust that exists on both sides. Painchaud said a feeling has developed among some officers that a lot of people in the black community have a persecution complex. "So, often, police officers who are accused of racism, they feel they are victimized."

For his part, Wortley believes police officers often feel if a person doesn't do anything wrong, the justice system won't hurt them.

"They don't realize the psychological damage it (frequent stops) has on individuals. It's a constant reminder that race still matters."

3

Racial Profiling Is a Symptom of a Larger Disease in the United States

Richard Thompson Ford

Richard Thompson Ford, a graduate of Harvard Law School, has been a member of the Stanford Law faculty since 1994. An authority on civil rights and antidiscrimination laws, Ford also has worked as a housing policy consultant in Cambridge, Massachusetts, and as commissioner of public housing in San Francisco. He has authored several books about race and has written on the subject of race and multiculturalism for several major newspapers.

The well-publicized July 2009 incident between renowned Harvard African-American scholar Henry Louis Gates Jr. and a white Cambridge police sergeant proved that whenever high-profile cases of possible racial discrimination or police brutality are brought to the public's attention, the controversy begets a never-ending cycle of mutual accusation and denial. Effective ways to end this cycle are elusive and may never be found until our society becomes more equal, as a whole.

As many of us learned early this week, Henry Louis Gates Jr., the eminent Harvard scholar of African-American culture, was arrested a week ago [July 16, 2009] outside his own home in Cambridge, Mass. Gates had returned home after an overseas trip and found his front door was jammed. He forced it open with the help of his driver. One of his neighbors saw the men forcing the door and called the police to report a burglary. When the police arrived and demanded that Gates come outside (or "asked" depending on which account of events you believe), Gates refused and a confrontation ensued, which ended in Gates being placed under arrest for disorderly conduct.

Racial profiling has become a sort of catchall term: If the police consider race in any way, it's profiling.

Reactions were swift and predictable: For liberal civil rights activists, Gates was a victim of racial profiling. For law-and-order conservatives, Gates is a pampered black elitist who played the race card against a hardworking cop who was just trying to do his job (and said today that he won't apologize, as Gates has asked). Neither of these reactions offers much insight into Gates' arrest or how we can prevent similar episodes in the future. Instead, both play into the all-too-familiar pattern of every racial scandal in recent memory: a depressing cycle of racial accusation, denial, and recrimination, in which the arguments all have been made many times before, and everyone knows which side they're on before even hearing the facts.

Last night [July 22] even the president [Barack Obama] weighed in, saying police acted "stupidly" by arresting Gates. Strong words, but Obama in his typically diplomatic style was careful to say he couldn't tell what role race played in the incident. The president got it right: There's no plausible justification for the arrest. It was worse than stupid—it was abusive. And that raises the suspicion that it was racially motivated. But there's really no evidence that the police officer involved was a racist rather than a bully with a badge or a decent cop who made a bad call in the heat of the moment.

Is "Racial Profiling" an Over-used Term?

Let's take the charge of racial profiling first. Strictly speaking, there was no profiling here: Sgt. James Crowley did not assume that professor Gates was a burglar because he fit some generic stereotype of a black criminal; he was responding to a 911 call. But racial profiling has become a sort of catchall term: If the police consider race in any way, it's profiling. The claim here is that once the police arrived, they treated Gates differently than they would have treated a white person in the same situation. It's clear that Sgt. Crowley, who arrived at Gates' home last Thursday, treated Gates as a suspect: He demanded that Gates step outside, and when Gates said he lived there, the officer demanded identification.

Was this racist? The witness who called 911 said that two black men were breaking into the house, so it wasn't outrageous for Crowley to suspect that the black man he saw inside the house had just broken in. If there was racial profiling, it began with the neighbor who described the burglary suspects in terms of race (or the 911 operator who probably prompted her to do so). But that's a normal part of a suspect description: Like sex, height, and weight, race is a convenient way to identify a person. Asking police to ignore race in a description of a specific suspect takes colorblindness way too far.

Many police officers demand more than orderly conduct; they demand submission and deference.

Statistics Lead to Stereotyping and Misguided Behaviors

And even racial profiling in the sense of using race as a part of a generic composite of a typical criminal isn't necessarily racist. It's a tragic fact that blacks as a group commit a disproportionate number of certain types of crime. The trouble is that racial profiling—even if it's based on accurate generalizations—imposes a disproportionate share of the costs of law enforcement on innocent blacks, like professor Gates. Let's face it: It's hard to imagine that police would have presumed that a middle-aged white man who walks with a cane was a burglar.

Still, the larger problem wasn't that Crowley considered Gates' race in assessing whether he might be a burglar. It's what Crowley did after learning that Gates was the lawful occupant of the house. And this is where the idea that Crowley was a cop just trying to do his job and Gates a spoiled black Brahmin playing the race card doesn't wash. The details are contested (and of course, the details are everything). According to the police report, Sgt. Crowley "asked" Gates to step outside and he refused. The report states that after Gates produced his identification, Crowley left and that Gates followed Crowley outside to berate him for racism. But Gates says he asked for Crowley's name and badge number, as is his right under Massachusetts law, and Crowley refused to provide them. Then Gates followed the officer outside and at some point said (or yelled) "Is this how you treat a black man in America?" Everyone agrees that this is when Crowley arrested Gates for "disorderly conduct."

Tense Situations Result in Uncharacteristic Reactions

I know Gates and find it very hard to imagine him engaged in "disorderly conduct." But many police officers demand more than orderly conduct; they demand submission and deference. Given the difficult and dangerous jobs they do, they usually deserve it. But it would be naive to imagine that there are no power-hungry bigots wearing the uniform. Anyone, particularly a black person, needs only to encounter one such rogue officer to find himself in serious jeopardy—at that point a few hours in custody is about the best one can hope for. Maybe

Gates, who is well-acquainted with the history of American racism, raised his voice in anger or fear. Maybe he even unfairly berated Crowley. But there's no way that the slight, 58-year-old Harvard scholar, with his cane, posed a threat to public order that justified his arrest.

Neither the overused notion of racial profiling nor the trope of a black malcontent playing the race card gives us any real purchase on this controversy.

I don't know whether Crowley arrested Gates because he was angry that an uppity black man dared to question him or whether this was just a tense misunderstanding that escalated out of control. What's clear is that neither the overused notion of racial profiling nor the trope of a black malcontent playing the race card gives us any real purchase on this controversy. Gates has said he hopes to use the incident as a teaching moment. But if we are really to learn anything from it, we'll have to look deeper. We need to ask why so many police officers of all races suspect the worst of racial minorities. (I wonder what the black Cambridge police officer pictured in the photo along with Gates after his arrest would say about all of this if he could speak candidly.) Decades of blatant and pervasive racial discrimination, poor urban planning, and failed labor policy have left blacks disproportionately jobless and trapped in poor ghettos across the United States. Faced with few opportunities and few positive role models, a disturbing number of people in those neighborhoods turn to gangs and crime for money, protection, and esteem.

It Is Easier to Assess Blame than to Address the Problem

Rather than improve those neighborhoods and help the people who live in them join the prosperous mainstream, we as a society have given police the dirty job of quarantining them.

Frankly, we should expect that a disproportionate number of power-hungry bigots would find such a mandate attractive. And an otherwise decent and fair-minded officer, faced with the day-to-day task of controlling society's most isolated, desperate, and angry population, might develop some ugly racial generalizations and carry them even to plush and leafy neighborhoods such as those surrounding Harvard Yard. Yet when the inevitable racial scandal surfaces we, like Capt. Renault in *Casablanca*, are shocked, shocked to find racial bias in law enforcement and quick to blame individual police officers, rather than ourselves.

The baseless arrest of one of the nation's most esteemed scholars is wrong and unfortunate, whether racism or simple abuse of authority is to blame. Professor Gates was publicly humiliated and spent several hours confined in a jail cell for, at most, asserting himself against a mistaken policeman. He deserves the apology he has asked for and apparently won't receive. But the larger problem of racial disparity in law enforcement is not caused by individual misconduct, and it will not be solved by apologies extracted under pressure or the threat of litigation. It's a symptom of the way we have chosen to deal with poverty and racial isolation in this very wealthy and supposedly egalitarian society. And it makes all police scapegoats for the failed and callous social policies that we have all chosen or acquiesced to.

4

Abuse of Authority May Be Mistaken as Racial Profiling

Sandy Banks

Sandy Banks has held various writing and editorial positions with the Los Angeles Times.

In a case such as the Henry Louis Gates Jr./James Crowley incident in Cambridge, Massachusetts, on July 16, 2009, the whistle most quickly blown by the public tends to focus on the perceived penalty of racial discrimination. However, it would be more appropriate—and perhaps a better way to bond races together—to call for an end to abusive law enforcement practices. Rather than reduce the issue to a timeworn black-versus-white controversy, the Gates/Crowley matter should be reviewed along the stronger lines of misuse of authority, which has an equally negative effect on everybody.

I can already envision the hate mail this column will generate. Every time I write about anything involving race, my inbox fills with invective—racial slurs, rants about the "welfare crowd," suggestions that I stop whining, go back to Africa and turn my "affirmative action job" over to some slighted white person.

So I know a bit about how Cambridge, Mass., Police Sgt. James Crowley must have felt when he was insulted by Harvard professor Henry Louis Gates Jr. after showing up to investigate a possible break-in at the professor's home.

Being accused of racism hurts, makes you want to fight back. My job requires that I not be goaded into incivility, because it's not my personal honor hanging on my response, but the reputation of my newspaper and the dignity of my profession.

I wish Crowley had thought of that during his public face-off [on July 16, 2009] with Professor Gates.

We don't know all the details of their encounter, but what began with Gates trying to dislodge his jammed front door ended with the 58-year-old African American scholar in handcuffs, under arrest for being—according to Crowley's police report—"loud and tumultuous."

The disorderly conduct charge was dropped, but the stain it left seems destined to spread. The incident has reignited a national debate over racial profiling, and even drawn the president [Barack Obama] into the back-and-forth.

But this is not as simple as black suspect, white cop. And race might not be the bottom line.

Police Officer's Actions Caused Escalation

I was angry when I first heard the news. If "Skip" Gates—prominent scholar, author and friend of Barack Obama—can be arrested on his own front porch simply for mouthing off to a cop, then the rest of us "loud and tumultuous" black folks surely better stay inside.

Being accused of racism hurts, makes you want to fight back.

Then I cringed when I read the officer's account of Gates' alleged tirade, riddled with the kind of "yo' momma" insults we used to trade on the school playground. I could feel Gates' fury, and imagine Crowley feeling bound to flex his power.

According to the police report, Crowley had been summoned by someone who thought Gates was breaking into the home. Gates seemed incensed by the presumption and was initially uncooperative.

But once Gates produced his driver's license and Harvard ID, it seems to me the officer's job was done. No crime, no suspect, no need to hang around.

Instead, the scene escalated. Gates began yelling for the officer's name and badge number; Crowley ordered the professor onto the porch. Gates called Crowley racially biased; Crowley warned him to calm down and unsnapped his handcuffs.

That's when the officer's actions turned a minor altercation into a national drama.

Police Authority Must Be Used with Discretion

The story resonates here in Los Angeles, where the Police Department is finally shedding its generations-old reputation for callous treatment of minorities and general rudeness to civilians. The department still has a ways to go; hundreds of racial profiling complaints have been filed in recent years, and the LAPD [Los Angeles Police Department] has not considered a single one valid.

But at least our cops are more civil when they pull you over.

"It's always a better outcome when you can resolve a situation by using as little of your authority as possible."

That's by design, said Capt. Bill Scott, a 20-year veteran who commands the northeast San Fernando Valley's Mission Division.

"We're training to have thick skin, not to take things personally," said Scott, a former training officer. "Even if the person you're dealing with is verbally attacking you, you can't react to that."

Encounters with police can be traumatic for reasons officers might not understand, he said. "If somebody's upset, you have to allow people some room to vent. There's an acceptable range of venting that's allowable and understandable."

Was Gates outside that range, I asked, with his alleged yelling and accusations of racism? "There's no perfect formula for what's allowable," Scott said. "It depends on what that officer was comfortable with. You just can't let it get to the point where somebody's safety is at risk."

I asked him if Crowley was on a power trip? "Without knowing all the facts," he said, "I don't want to be critical of that department and that officer."

But he was clear on something that every officer ought to remember.

At its heart, this is a power struggle that didn't have to happen.

"It's always a better outcome when you can resolve a situation by using as little of your authority as possible. And a lot of that is how you perceive the other side. . . . And whether you're willing to explain what you're doing. Instead of just issuing an order."

Respect for Authority and Respectful Use of Authority Go Hand in Hand

It would be naive to ignore the racial dimensions of this. A successful black man being interrogated in his own home, Gates may have seen the white cop as disrespectful. And Crowley, a well-regarded white officer, probably expected deference, not insults, from the black man he'd been called to help.

But at its heart, this is a power struggle that didn't have to happen. The police—as [Barack] Obama put it before he felt compelled to back off—acted stupidly.

I can see hands poised over keyboard now, ready to unleash a flood of e-mails. So here I go:

Professor Gates should have been more polite. The officer arrived to investigate a crime report. Gates may have had a legitimate gripe, but that does not excuse the rant described in Crowley's police report. Police officers deserve respect—just like teachers and grocery store clerks and even newspaper reporters.

Sgt. Crowley should have been able to defuse the situation without bringing the handcuffs out. I understand that police officers have a difficult job to do, but taking guff is part of the job description. A police department's reputation and success rest on the attitude of its officers.

We ought to stop seeing this as a referendum on racism and ask what it says about the attitude police officers display toward the taxpayers who fund their paychecks.

We rely for our safety on their good judgment. Yet every time I write about some cop embroiled in a controversy, I hear from people of every race—teenagers, housewives, businessmen—relaying stories of encounters with rude or unreasonable police.

In the end, this may not be at all about racial profiling, but about the line between dangerous defiance of police and mindless submission to authority. And whether being "loud and tumultuous" ought to land a righteously angry man behind bars.

5

Racial Profiling by Police Officers Invites Revenge

Nayaba Arevde

Nayaba Arevde writes for the New York Amsterdam News.

A seemingly unjustified shooting by New York Police Department (NYPD) officers that killed 23-year-old Sean Bell resulted in a retaliatory killing of NYPD officer Russell Timoschenko, which many in the African-American community applauded as an appropriate "eye-for-an-eye" response. Repeated charges of NYPD racial profiling and discrimination have led to a predictably tense community; the reverberations will continue unless and until the police change their tactics ... but is it already too late?

As one city cop is buried Thursday [July 19, 2007], Black residents, activists and concerned individuals are speaking about what may be an upcoming backlash.

Returning from police officer Russel Timoshenko's wake, Councilman Charles Barron told the *AmNews*, "We, of course, express our condolences to his family, who I met and embraced. But I hope that this tragedy does not lead to an enhancement of aggression and the terrorism that our community has suffered from New York City police officers."

"Despite what the media has put forward, we don't know the facts in this case," a New York attorney told the *AmNews* this week. "Nobody wants to touch the question as to why did they stop the car in the first place. Were they racially *profiling*?

Nayaba Arevde, "The Bell Still Tolls," *New York Amsterdam News*, vol. 98, July 19, 2007. Reproduced by permission.

"The bells of *racial* profiling and white supremacy are ringing," said Divine Allah, youth minister of the New Black Panther Party. "*Racial profiling* and the result of this racist bell ringing was what got these cops shot," he said bluntly. "But, we are still upset about the killing of Sean Bell, and we aren't going to let what happened last week overshadow what happened last November. Fifty shots. Sean was 23 years old."

"The bells of racial *profiling and white supremacy are ringing."*

As he prepared to officially announce his 2009 run for Brooklyn borough president on Sunday, Barron added, "Most Black people are decent law-abiding citizens, and we hope that the death of this officer does not act as a green light for other officers to seek some sort of revenge and increase the pain and suffering already experienced by Black families."

Hate-filled Rhetoric Calls for Action

A visit to the rabid NYPD [New York Police Department] Rant website, for example talks about: "NYC [New York City] Savages, you are all herby [sic] put on notice. To all you criminal scum out there, your' [sic] heroes Baron and Sharpton cant [sic] save you. You cant [sic] hide behind that 51 (sic) shot rhetoric anymore. Forget that 3 shot and asses [sic] too. ITS ON.

"WE ARE THE POLICE. AND IF YOU SHOOT AT US, WE WILL SHOOT AT YOU AND WE WILL CONTINUE TO SHOOT UNTIL THE THREAT IS OVER, REGARDLESS OF HOW MANY SHOTS IT TAKES. 1, 41, 51, 151, 251—AS MANY AS IT TAKES."

The blogger calling himself or herself "Ghetto Dawg" ran the mantra: "SHOOT FAST, SHOOT STRAIGHT AND SHOOT TO KILL. All this crap about being sensitive to the community and not intimidating anyone, and CPR nees [sic] to take a backseat to the our own safety, f.ck [sic] political correctness. Look out for number 1."

Police Response and Community Reactions Are Predictable

It is these types of overtones, plus street-corner testimonies, and personal or acquired knowledge of police abuse or misconduct, that is leading some people to assess that last Saturday's death of Timoshenko after being allegedly shot by two Black men, will give some cops a convenient reason for a vamped-up open season on many Black males.

"Each and every Black male should be on alert," said Divine Allah.

"If you're involved in a traffic stop, you need to pull over, roll your window down, and put your hands on the steering wheel," said Atty. [Attorney] Michael Hardy. "Then deal with the cops with respect, assuming they deal with you respectfully."

A law enforcer said that routine traffic stops were "standard," but many people in the Black community told the *Am-News* that outcome notwithstanding, they felt that *racial profiling* was a major factor.

"The Amsterdam News" asked the police department what prompted officers Herman Yan and Timoshenko to stop the dark-colored BMW allegedly with three Black men in it: the two accused shooters—Dexter Bostic and Robert Ellis—and Lee Woods. John Kelly from the police press office replied: "The license plates on the vehicle were registered to another vehicle."

However distant and far removed from the front, or even middle pages, the clatter of the NYPD 50-shot Bell barrage is still ringing in the ears of people of the NYC and the tri-state.

The wall-to-wall media coverage of the traffic stop; the shooting of cops Yan and Timoshenko; the major boots-on-the-ground, blood-hound-assisted, heavily armed hunt for the three suspects; and their objectivity-free, media-hailed capture brought out an interesting response from many in the Black community.

"When Eleanor Bumpers [a Black grandmother], was shot by a cop, they didn't cry for us," said activist and retired educator Dr. Jack Felder. "When that cop shot [unarmed 19-year-old] Timothy Stansbury in Brooklyn, they didn't cry for us; when they shot Sean Bell on his wedding day, they didn't cry for us, so what kind of fool do they take me for, thinking that I'm going to cry for them now?"

There Is No Good, or Positive, Outcome

Some folk in private and in published reports have expressed a desire for the same level of righteous indignation in the pursuit of justice come the Sean Bell trial, where three NYPD law enforcers will be on trial for his 50-shot shooting death.

Queens [N.Y.] D.A. [district attorney] Richard Brown's office did not respond to e-mail or phone requests for an update in the case. Atty. Michael Hardy, who is representing Nicole Paultre-Bell, Sean's "widow" told the AmNews, "As far as I know, there hasn't been any movement in the case. We are waiting for the defendants to file their motions, which they should have done in June. We should be in court on September 7 [2007] to hear a decision on their motion."

Atty. Michael Warren told the *AmNews* that the police beating and arrest of himself and his wife, Evelyn, on June 28 following their questioning cops battering a young Black male, illustrates the fact that no one is immune.

Warren, who was released after his arrest from the 77th Precinct only after 200-plus supporters showed up there to demand the Warrens be let out, added, "We will not allow the mayor or the police commissioner to use this unfortunate set of circumstances as a basis for the legitimization of further attacks on our communities of color."

Meanwhile, Allah noted, "Whether a cop has been on the force for 20 years or 18 months, when they walk down the block, they are like, 'I'm white and I've got a gun on my side—get out of my way, or do what I say. This arrogance and disrespect leads to *profiling*, which leads to brutality and harassment, and then murder. This time their government-endorsed racist tactics backfired.

"But, any way you look at it, the Black man ends up still a victim because now the racist antennae are all tuned in to that high-pitched racist frequency—which means that each and any Black man is on the radar and even more so is a target of a police department which will say because the death of one officer, the entire Black male population in particular, but Black people in general, still can and will be treated as suspect."

"There is something brewing in the Black communities around the nation."

The nine-month wake after Bell's death at the hands of three NYPD cops last November has done little to dissipate the anger in the community, Allah told the *AmNews*. "The bell is still ringing. There are people who are fired up because of the tragic police murder of Sean Bell."

Allah said that a feeling exists that the dam is about to burst.

There will [be] those who will respond with actions that benefit the mindset of a revolutionary; and there [be] will those who will respond with actions that benefit the white supremacist system, unfortunately.

To everything there is season, and to quote my elder comrade on the frontline, the honorable Charles Barron, "There is something brewing in the Black communities around the nation, not just New York.'"

6

The Media Presents Misleading Statistics on Racial Profiling by Police

Heather MacDonald

Heather MacDonald is a journalist who has written on various social issues including racism, immigration, homelessness, and poverty. Her work has appeared in the Washington Post, New York Times, *and* Wall Street Journal.

While reporting controversial incidents of alleged racial profiling by police officers, the media has an obligation to present the facts accurately. Reporters should present statistical data in such a manner as to reflect the full picture of such data—they should not "pick-and-choose" certain elements and thus skew the statistical findings. These responsibilities weigh particularly heavily on major, well-trusted media such as the New York Times, *whose journalistic standards are upheld as models for countless other news organizations throughout this country, as well as the world.*

The *New York Times*'s bad faith regarding the police has reached a new low. On August 24 [2005], a front-page article claimed that the Justice Department had tried to suppress damning evidence of racial profiling by the nation's police forces. In fact, it is the *Times* that is suppressing evidence.

For years, activists have argued that some drivers face a heightened risk of being stopped by bigoted cops. David Har-

Heather MacDonald, "Reporting While Wrong," *National Review*, vol. 57, September 26, 2005, p. 43–44. Copyright © 2005 by National Review, Inc., 215 Lexington Avenue, New York, NY 10016. Reproduced by permission.

ris, a University of Toledo law professor and ubiquitous police critic, provided a classic statement of the "Driving While Black" concept in 1999: "Anyone who is African-American is automatically suspect during every drive to work, the store, or a friend's house." Owing to this "automatic suspicion," Harris posited in his 2002 book, *Profiles in Injustice*, "pretextual stops will be used against African-Americans and Hispanics ... out of proportion to their numbers in the driving population."

Statistics Are Challenged

The "Driving While Black" belief is pervasive, powerful, and false. According to a survey of 80,000 civilians conducted by the Bureau of Justice Statistics [BJS] (an arm of the Justice Department) in 2002, an identical proportion of white, black, and Hispanic drivers—9 percent—were stopped by the police in the previous year. And the stop rate for blacks was lower during the day, when officers can more readily determine a driver's race, than at night. These results demolish the claim that minorities are disproportionately subject to "pretextual stops."

Criminology studies have long found that the greatest predictor of police behavior is civilian behavior.

Clearly, these findings should be news of a high order—so that must be why the *Times* buried them in paragraph 11 of its front-page story (and omitted the day-night disparity entirely). But not only did the *Times* conceal the study's import, it also had the temerity to spin the survey as *confirming* the racial-profiling myth. Indeed, the BJS study will "add grist to the debate over using racial and ethnic data in law enforcement," the newspaper asserted, because it provided evidence of "the aggressive police treatment of black and Hispanic drivers."

Prejudice Not Proven

What is this evidence for racist policing, in the paper's view? The *Times* bases its charge on two findings from the survey: According to driver self-reports, blacks and Hispanics were more likely to have their persons or cars searched than white drivers, and were more likely to be subjected to the threat or use of force by the officer who stopped them. The survey defines force as pushing, grabbing, or hitting; a typical force incident, characterized by the survey respondent as "excessive," consisted of an officer grabbing the respondent by the arm as he was fleeing the scene and pushing him against his car. Specifically, black drivers said that they or their cars were searched 10.2 percent of the time following a stop, Hispanic drivers 11.4 percent of the time, and white drivers 3.5 percent of the time. As for police threats or use of force, 2.4 percent of Hispanic drivers, 2.7 percent of black drivers, and 0.8 percent of white drivers claimed that force had been threatened or used against them.

Blacks and Hispanics have been fed a steady diet of police-racism stories.

None of these findings establishes prejudicial treatment of minorities. The *Times*, for instance, does not reveal that blacks and Hispanics were far more likely to be *arrested* following a stop: Blacks were 11 percent of all stopped drivers, but 24 percent of all arrested drivers; Hispanics, 9.5 percent of all stopped drivers, but 18.4 percent of all arrested drivers; and whites, 76.5 percent of all stopped drivers, but 58 percent of arrested drivers. The higher black and Hispanic arrest rates undoubtedly result from their higher crime rates. The national black murder rate, for example, is seven times higher than that of all other races combined, and the black robbery rate eight times higher. Though the FBI [Federal Bureau of Investigation] does not keep national crime data on Hispanics, lo-

cal police statistics usually put the Hispanic crime rate between the black and white crime rates. These differential crime
rates mean that when the police run a computer search on
black and Hispanic drivers following a stop, they are far more
likely to turn up outstanding arrest warrants than for white
drivers.

Past Criminal Records Are Presently Damaging

These higher arrest rates in turn naturally result in higher
search rates: Officers routinely search civilians incident to an
arrest. Moreover, the higher crime rates among blacks and
Hispanics mean a greater likelihood that evidence of a crime,
such as weapons or drugs, may be in plain view, thereby trig-
gering an arrest and a search.

The higher incidence of police threats or use of force
against blacks and Hispanics—assuming the self-reports are
accurate—is also more likely to result from driver conduct
than from police bias. Criminology studies have long found
that the greatest predictor of police behavior is civilian behavior. Threaten or challenge an officer and you are likely to be
challenged back. The 2002 BJS survey concluded that persons
who provoked the police were significantly more likely to experience the threat or use of force by the officer than persons
who did not. Thus, 24 percent of persons involved in a police
force incident admitted to cursing at, insulting, or threatening
the officer. The number of people who *actually* engaged in
such behavior is probably higher still.

Media Racist Rhetoric Leads to Resistance

Speculatively speaking, it is likely that a greater percentage of
blacks and Hispanics challenged or threatened a police officer
than did whites. Why? Because for the last decade and a half,
blacks and Hispanics have been fed a steady diet of police-
racism stories. They have been told again and again that if an

officer stops them, it is because of their race, not their conduct. Police officers have come to expect that the first words out of a black driver's mouth following a traffic stop will be, "You only stopped me because I'm black." The chance that such an attitude will escalate into more hostile behavior is much greater than zero. In addition, the differential crime rates mean that a higher proportion of black and Hispanic drivers will have a crime in their past that could lead them to resist the officer making the stop.

The BJS authors explicitly disavowed the possibility of using the survey data to conclude that driver race, rather than conduct, resulted in different search or force rates. The *Times*, however, shows no such reluctance. After belatedly acknowledging the identical stop rates among different racial and ethnic groups, the paper hastens to add that "what happened once the police made a stop differed markedly depending on race and ethnicity." The *Times* then goes on to posit a [George W.] Bush administration cover-up of these allegedly compromising findings. According to the *Times*'s narrative, political appointees in the Justice Department demoted the Bureau of Justice Statistics director, Lawrence Greenfeld, after he refused to delete references to the differential search and force rates from a press release announcing the 2002 survey. And in a further manifestation of political meddling, per the paper, the Justice Department opted not to issue the contested press release at all, but simply posted the report online—as it has done for nearly 70 percent of the reports released in 2004 and 2005. That was another detail not disclosed in the *Times*'s story.

The *Times* Must Take Responsibility

So what? A press release that focused on the search and arrest rates would be seriously misleading. Yet the *Times*'s fake scoop produced the usual reaction: eager mimicry. Within 24 hours, news outlets ranging from National Public Radio to the *St. Pe-*

tersburg Times had reproduced the story. One career cop-basher, Rep. John Conyers of Michigan, called for a congressional investigation into the alleged "cover-up." And the NAACP [National Association for the Advancement of Colored People] claimed that the study confirmed the "truth about racial profiling."

The drumbeat against the cops increases the hostility against them.

The notion that the police target blacks and Hispanics because of their skin color has damaged urban life. Thanks to racial-data-collection mandates, every officer knows that if he has "too many" interactions with minority citizens—including responding to crime calls or preventing a mugging—he could face a bias charge. Some officers will decide that it's wiser for their careers not to fight crime aggressively, leaving law-abiding inner-city residents at the mercy of thugs. The drumbeat against the cops increases the hostility against them, poisoning the trust needed for the most effective police work. The *New York Times*'s endless crusade against phantom police racism ensures that the poorest neighborhoods will continue to be held back by fear and violence.

7

Racial Profiling Is Legitimate and Necessary to Ensure Security

John Winn

John Winn has served in the U.S. Army Judge Advocate General (JAG) Corps, which included five years on the Law Faculty at West Point (the U.S. Military Academy) in New York. He currently teaches business and constitutional law at Shenandoah University in Winchester, Virginia.

Although racial profiling in itself seems wrong, those who are charged with ensuring our national security have a duty of vigilance over certain groups or types of individuals who have proven particularly hostile toward our country. We would be remiss to allow potential charges of profiling to prevent us from taking every reasonable step to ensure everyone's safety to the fullest extent possible.

In light of the attempted Christmas Day [2009] bombing aboard Northwest Airlines Flight 253, it was certainly appropriate that President [Barack] Obama directed a review of airline screening policies and procedures.

It is unlikely, however, that the current administration will re-evaluate long-standing policies prohibiting ethnic or gender-based terror profiling.

Nevertheless, failure to make common-sense changes may increase the chance that persons like Nigerian Umar Farouk

John Winn, "The Legitimacy in Profiling; A Dereliction in Overlooking the Obvious," *The Washington Times*, December 30, 2009. Reproduced by permission.

Abdulmutallab or "shoe-bomber" Richard Reid (aka Abdul Raheem) will one day succeed in detonating a bomb aboard a commercial aircraft.

Considering the explosive power of PETN (the explosive apparently utilized in both incidents), we can count ourselves as extraordinarily lucky that no American lives have been lost in such an attack thus far.

Accusations of Profiling Hinder Security Concerns

Unfortunately, political correctness and misguided past applications of racial profiling by domestic law enforcement have poisoned the profiling well in the war on terrorism (or whatever the Obama administration calls its counterterrorism policy this month).

While ethnic minorities are statistically no more likely than whites to violate domestic laws, 32 of the 45 groups recognized as "foreign terrorist organizations" by the State Department are Islamist in orientation with direct ties to the Middle East, the Arabian Gulf region, Africa or South Asia.

Over the previous 25 years, Islamist "jihadism" has become the primary global threat to democratic values, peace and stability. With few, but certainly notable exceptions, the foot soldiers of terror attacks are primarily young men of Middle Eastern, North African or South Asian backgrounds. Most are in good physical health, well-educated, speak several languages, and are (outwardly at least) fairly well-adjusted. Many have either lived in or were born in the West.

Those who assert profiling is always wrong, even if effective, rarely find themselves in positions of responsibility for the safety and security of others.

Regrettably, if as a society America accepts profiling, we appear to endorse practices that seem fundamentally unfair and discriminatory. But, complete or perfect "fairness" is impossible when dealing with terrorists and terrorism. In an age of malevolent terror directed almost exclusively against innocents, there is something hopelessly derelict about ignoring race, gender and ethnicity (among other factors) in our national security strategy. Those who assert profiling is always wrong, even if effective, rarely find themselves in positions of responsibility for the safety and security of others.

Most travelers routinely expect close security for almost any reason at all.

Profiling Is Understandable, but Controversial

Few people realize that under limited circumstances, security screening based at least in part upon ethnic or gender profiling violates neither constitutional protections nor federal civil rights laws.

Limited profiling is compatible with the president's War Powers under Article II and with implied executive powers granted by Congress after Sept. 11, 2001. Within this context, most travelers routinely expect close scrutiny for almost any reason at all. Surveys consistently indicate terrorism the most important issue of concern to Americans and polling conducted in 2002 by Public Agenda revealed that two-thirds of Americans "agreed that racial profiling of Middle-Easterners by law enforcement is understandable" (although of course regrettable).

Current [2003] Justice Department guidelines regarding the use of race by federal law enforcement agencies quite appropriately state that linking racial characteristics "misconduct" is "erroneous," "ineffective," and "harmful" to society. With respect to national (and border) security, the guidelines state that federal agents "may not consider race or ethnicity except the extent permitted by the Constitution and laws of the United States." This is the equivalent of proclaiming that "profiling is not authorized unless it is authorized."

To add to this confusion, in a footnote, the guidelines declare that "officials involved in homeland security may take into account specific, credible information about the descriptive characteristics of persons who are affiliated with identified organizations that are actively engaged in threatening the national security."

Common Sense and Experience Are the Best Security Tools

To insist that an experienced bomb-dog handler or baggage screener, ignore any hunches while mindlessly sticking to random passenger screening is, at best, a waste of limited resources. Sky marshals, Transportation Security Administration screeners, and others on the front lines of counterterrorism should be afforded sufficient discretion to draw upon their common sense and experience regarding people who exhibit nonbehavioral risk factors.

Protecting our values, however, requires balancing zeal with caution.

While racial or gender-based profiling should never be considered acceptable under all circumstances, future guidance should take into consideration real-world threats while ensuring that valid cultural sensitivities are respected.

In his message on Monday [December 28, 2009], the president promised to "do everything in our power to protect our country." He also said his administration "will be guided by our hopes, our unity, and our deeply held values."

Bravo, as a great nation our strength derives, in large part, from our cultural and ethnic diversity. Protecting our values, however, requires balancing zeal with caution. While we zealously face the threat of Islamist terror, we should be free to carry out policies that involve brief and typically trivial impositions upon persons who, unfortunately, share some of the outward appearances of our enemies.

8

Racial Profiling Is Less Important than Other Security Measures

Michael Chertoff

Michael Chertoff was secretary of the U.S. Department of Home-land Security from February 2005 to January 2009.

Authorities in the United States and abroad have been proactive in taking steps to ensure the safety of airline passengers. Although safety has to be the number one priority, measures can, and should, be taken to also safeguard passenger conveniences.

Traveling by plane in the USA, especially in the wake of the disrupted London airliner bombing plot earlier this month [August 2006], looks nothing like it did before the 9/11 [2001] attacks. Liquids or gels aren't allowed in carry-ons (with a few exceptions). The rules have adapted to emerging threats (remember when nail files were forbidden?). Shoe removal is required at every airport. Air marshals have become frequent fliers, and your pilot might be armed with a gun. The government also moved to centralize the defense of the nation with the creation of the Department of Homeland Security. Its secretary, Michael Chertoff, discussed air security and other issues with *USA Today*'s editorial board. His comments were edited for length and clarity.

"The 'Why' Behind Air Security; Chertoff Explains Why He Opposes Racial Profiling, Supports the Ban on Liquids and Considers Fliers' Convenience in Making Decisions," in *USA Today*, August 31, 2006, p. 11A. Reproduced by permission.

USA Today: The terrorism threat comes predominantly from young, Muslim male extremists. Without racial or ethnic profiling, are there ways to make airport security better match this threat?

Michael Chertoff: Yes. At the extreme, 3-year-olds are not probably a threat we need to worry about, and 75-year-old grandmothers are probably not a threat. But if you look at the experience of watching suicide bombers in other parts of the world, saying those can't be women is just not factually correct. So I'm hesitant to say that we should focus only on males, or Muslims of a particular age.

Profiling Is Not Only Wrong, It Also Is Not Enough

So what might an airport screener look for?

We are training our screening officers in behavioral pattern recognition, looking at ways people behave that will actually suggest they're trying to hide something. That's a positive step that does not require ethnic profiling but looks to the pattern of behavior. I think some element of that is talking to people when they come through, asking them a few basic questions: Where are you going? What are you doing? Why are you going there? These are tools that would allow us to be more precise, but without getting into racial profiling, which is a bad thing.

The trick for us is to find a system that keeps out bad stuff and is as efficient and as convenient as possible.

Have you learned any more about the chemistry of the London plot that might enable you to fine-tune the ban on liquids and gels?

The chemistry's still being looked at. But I actually want to come at it a different way. The question becomes not only is there a more precise way to screen out liquids you're worried about, the question is whether doing so would actually be more inconvenient than having an absolute ban. There is technology that would allow you to screen—bottle by bottle—whether something is dangerous. The problem is that it takes a long time. If everybody carries four bottles and it takes 15 seconds, that's a minute per person. Well, if you have 300 people boarding a jet, that's 300 minutes to board. Nobody wants to do that. The trick for us is to find a system that keeps out bad stuff and is as efficient and as convenient as possible. And sometimes it turns out that a more comprehensive ban is clearer, more easy to enforce and more efficient for the traveler.

Had you identified the threat of liquids before the London plot and considered how to combat it?

We were aware of this as an issue, and what was particularly troubling about this scheme is how hard these guys worked to come up with ways to conceal liquids. That is what made us see the need to go to this total ban. I had actually thought of a total ban, but I had a real concern about whether it was something that would work. What alarmed me about this was that it was a very, very sophisticated way to bring components in.

What role, if any, did the National Security Agency (NSA) terrorist surveillance program or the banking surveillance program play in thwarting the British terror plot?

I can just tell you at a very general level, the ability to monitor communications, or movement of money, is in my experience the single most important tool in stopping terrorist attacks. It's a very important tool.

There is a very obvious security gap regarding a less stringent screening of cargo shipments that are placed on passenger planes. Why has this not been a bigger priority?

It is a big priority. First, if you come to the airport or you go to the airline and you want to ship a package on a particular airline in the passenger hold, it's going to go through screening the same as a checked bag will. So people who say we don't screen that are just wrong. Now the (shipping companies) have to verify the person who's bringing the package in. Most of the FedEx and UPS stuff that the ordinary person sends doesn't go on passenger airlines. And I do think that the threat to cargo jets blowing up is not one that I think is probably a likely terrorist target given what we currently know.

But what if someone landed a low-level job at a known shipper? Isn't that still a vulnerability?

Here's the problem they would have. They would really have no way of knowing in advance whether a particular package would wind up on a passenger plane. So as a threat vector, it would be hard for somebody to plan, to be able to put something on a passenger jet. Now, that's not to say that we don't want to make it tougher. But the idea that anybody can come up and stick something in a passenger plane and know it's going to go there is actually not true.

Registering Travelers Might Increase Security

The Registered Traveler program, which asks passengers to volunteer information ahead of time, would smooth the screening process in exchange for faster screening, yet it hasn't happened. Why?

The airline industry at some point in the last year became somewhat less enthused about Registered Traveler because I think they came to the conclusion that it actually was not going to be something a lot of people would sign up for. I disagree with that. Frankly, there are privacy advocates who are strongly against it. We need to obviously make sure that we're obeying the privacy rules, but I think a Registered Traveler and some form of domestic Secure Flight (a similar government-sponsored program) is still the way to go. It still is better to get a little more information about people, and certainly on a voluntary basis, and then not have to put them into secondary (searches) than to put more people into secondary and have their stuff searched and have them asked questions.

What we'd want to do would actually enhance civil liberties.

Will the flying public embrace such voluntary screening?

Those who choose to do it will get the benefit of it and those who choose not to can weigh their own convenience.

There are significant civil liberties concerns associated with the war on terror as the government collects more and more information about its citizens. What will protect Americans from an encroachment by government in the future?

What we'd want to do would actually enhance civil liberties. For example, if we had more specific information about travel history and things of that sort—this is not deep secret stuff, this is stuff that you give to your travel agent—that data allows us to focus on people that we are really more worried about. I actually view that as a plus to civil liberties. I dare say if you asked most people, they'd rather give you a little more information and avoid getting patted down and having their bags gone through than have no information given out so we'd have to wind up doing searches of everybody.

No Cause for Complacency

'Constantly vigilant': Obviously, we are happy that there has not been a successful attack on the United States soil since 9/11, but that is not a cause for complacency. It's a cause for redoubled effort. Because I think it would be foolish to presume that that's going to continue forever. We will only avoid an attack if we are not only constantly vigilant but always adaptable in trying to look around the corner and see not only what happened before but what's going to happen next.

'A great deterrent': The big danger is the unknown terrorist, or the unidentified terrorist. And these guys leave fingerprints. They leave them on bomb fragments, they leave them in training camps, they leave them in apartments where terrorist planning takes place. We capture these. If we have 10-finger prints from everyone seeking to enter the country, we can run them against each other. The real beauty of this is, it's a great deterrent because now, as this gets rolled out over the next couple of years, every terrorist is going to have to ask himself, "Did I ever leave a fingerprint in a safe house or on some artifact that was found in a battlefield." And they're going to know that if they did, and they come across that border, we can catch them.

The challenge is to proceed in a way that will get us a balanced approach to security.

'The odds are against us': At Homeland Security, we have to bat a thousand. We have to stop everything. And particularly as you get into low-level, homegrown types of plots that don't require much planning, the odds are against us. A lone wolf can work without ever dealing with other people. It's going to be very hard to detect those.

'We can't go back': We need to get in a place that we can sustain over a long period of time. That means not overreaction, but also, not underreaction. We can't live in a state of constant paranoia or a feeling that we're in an armed camp because that would not be a sustainable way to lead our lives, and it would cause enormous damage to our freedoms. But we also can't go back to pre-Sept. 11 thinking, that these matters are going to take care of themselves and we do not have to adjust the way we live to take account of this very significant, ongoing threat. So the challenge is to proceed in a way that will get us a balanced approach to security—finding ways to be more precise in targeting the threat and eliminating it, with less inconvenience to innocent people and less disruption of our daily lives.

9

Profiling Muslims Will Not End Terrorism

Aziz Huq

Aziz Huq is the director of the Brennan Center for Justice's liberty and national security project.

Ever since the September 11, 2001, terrorist attacks, airlines have increased their vigilance, particularly targeting Muslim passengers. Whenever acts of terrorism are attempted, the call for profiling in the skies rises to even higher levels. This escalation, concentrating on airline security, will result in higher resentment on the part of Muslims, and will not deter terrorists.

We're all familiar by now with the theme song, even if this year it's being sung in a different key: an attempt at terrorism thwarted; calls for racial profiling go up.

Despite castigation from the right for being too soft on Muslims, the Transportation Security Agency (TSA) installed new search rules in late December [2009] for travelers from 14 mostly Muslim countries. Just as after September 11, 2001, the attempted bombing by Richard Reid and the 2006 arrests of more than 20 men allegedly involved in a transatlantic bombing conspiracy in the United Kingdom, blatant racial and religious profiling at our airports and borders seems just a question of time.

Racial Profiling Often Is Legislated

The use of racial or ethnic profiling is, in fact, nothing new in the United States. The earliest significant federal use of racial profiling was the 1882 Chinese Immigration Act, which dramatically constricted labor flows from Asia, as well as imposing harsh restrictions upon Chinese already in the United States. Indeed, some of the U.S. Supreme Court's earliest decisions on race under the Equal Protection Clause were responses to overt anti-Asian bigotry.

The 1924 Johnson-Reed Act then imposed national origin quotas designed to preserve the Caucasian tincture of the day. And in 2002, the so-called "special registration" program—an administrative venture the [President George W.] Bush-era INS [Immigration and Naturalization Service] imposed before any congressional authorization occurred—singled out citizens of majority Muslim countries (and, just for larks, North Korea) for special scrutiny.

American Muslims are often targeted for discriminatory searches of laptops and other personal property.

This year's [2010] racial profiling model is but the most recent in a long line of immigration measures grounded in dubious intelligence all too often based on ethnic and racial stereotypes.

Racial Profiling Is Not Always Legislated

It would be a mistake, though, to think that race only enters the equation through formal rules and directives. Last year, the San Francisco-based organization Muslim Advocates published an important study of Muslim Americans' experience with invasive and inappropriate questioning about faith and personal politics as they entered the U.S. As Sen. Russ Feingold has pointedly noted in Senate questioning of TSA [Transportation Security Administration] staff, American Muslims are often targeted for discriminatory searches of laptops and other personal property.

The new TSA rules, then, must be seen against the backdrop of an air travel security system that is already deeply racialized.

There is no evidence that racial or ethnic profiling decreases the net amount of terrorism.

None of this will especially surprise readers who have experienced first-hand mistreatment while traveling. It is, indeed, easy to despair that even eight years after the Sept. 11 attacks, we are still having the same conversation about race, security and justice. Yet progressives should not lose hope. In the last eight years, scholars and advocates have identified an increasing volume of evidence of profiling's failure—and, indeed, its harms to security goals. The Christmas day [2009] bombing attempt on an airplane traveling from Amsterdam to Detroit provides an opportunity to brush up on those arguments.

Profiling Actually Can Increase Terrorism

There is no evidence that racial or ethnic profiling decreases the net amount of terrorism. To the contrary, studies of airline security measures imposed after a wave of hijackings in the 1970s suggest that it has the perverse effect of increasing terrorism. In one of the best of these studies, Walter Enders and Todd Sandler found in 1993 that although new mandatory screening procedures decreased the number of hijackings, they coincided with an increase in other forms of terrorism, such as kidnappings and attacks on stationary targets.

10

Muslims Must Work to Dispel Erroneous Views About Islam

Abduljalil Sajid

Abduljalil Sajid is a member of the Central Working Committee of Great Britain and is vice chair of the United Kingdom Chapter of the World Conference of Religions for Peace.

Suggested by the term xenophobia, *which refers to a fear of anyone foreign or different, "Islamophobia" has become epidemic in the wake of September 11, 2001, and other Muslim-sanctioned acts of terror. Whenever the fanatic, lawless minority is given continual media scrutiny and censure, the majority of Muslims, peace-loving and law-abiding, suffer the same phobic consequences. Therefore, it is the duty of "good" followers of Islam to plant the seeds of understanding and acceptance among those of other faiths so as to encourage a more stable and harmonious relationship among all.*

The term "Islamophobia" is, admittedly, not ideal. It was coined by way of analogy to "xenophobia" and can be characterized by the belief that all or most Muslims are religious fanatics, have violent tendencies towards non-Muslims, and reject such concepts as equality, tolerance, and democracy. It is a new form of racism whereby Muslims, an ethno-religious group, not a race, are, nevertheless, constructed as a race. A set of negative assumptions are made of the entire group to the detriment of members of that group. During the

1990s many sociologists and cultural analysts observed a shift in racist ideas from ones based on skin color to ones based on notions of cultural superiority and otherness.

Manifestations of Hostility

In Britain as in other European or Western countries, manifestations of anti-Muslim hostility can be seen to include such features as verbal and physical attacks on Muslims in public places, and attacks on mosques and desecration of Muslim cemeteries. It can be seen in widespread and routine negative stereotyping in the media and everyday discourse in ways that would not be acceptable if the reference were, for example, to Jewish or black people; or in negative stereotypes and remarks in speeches by political leaders, implying that Muslims are less committed than others to democracy and the rule of law—the claim in Britain, for example, that Muslims must choose between "the British way" and "the terrorist way." It can also manifest itself in discrimination in recruitment and employment practices and in the workplace; in delay and inertia in responding to Muslim requests for cultural sensitivity in education, in healthcare, and in protection against incitement to hatred; and in curtailment of civil liberties that disproportionately affect Muslims.

A high proportion of refugees and people seeking asylum are Muslims.

Violent Language Against and Amid Muslims

September 11, 2001, and the days that followed produced strong feelings among non-Muslims as well as among Muslims. When people feel powerless and frustrated they are prone to hit out with violent language: "You don't belong here," or "Get out of my country now; England is for white civilized

English people!" are examples of the kind of violent language that was used in e-mail messages to the Muslim Council of Britain immediately following the attacks. These messages are significant, for they expressed attitudes and perceptions that are widespread amongst non-Muslims and that are recurring components of Islamophobia.

An alleged factor, some argue, that fuels Islamophobia is the rise of anti-Western Islamist movements, which have either come to power outright in some countries (Iran, Sudan, post-Soviet-era Afghanistan), or else exert a strong influence on government policy in others (Saudi Arabia, Pakistan). Many people mistakenly believe that most Muslims are Islamist, when in fact the Islamist movement is only a minority position. Perhaps the most important factor shaping the present wave of Islamophobia, though, is the extremely large and disproportionate media coverage given to Islamist-inspired terrorism, like the September 11 attacks, while relatively little media coverage is given to equivalent acts of terrorism by other groups or nation-states.

Contextual Factors Are Disadvantageous to Muslims

Islamophobia is heightened by a number of contextual factors. One of these is the fact that a high proportion of refugees and people seeking asylum are Muslims. Demonization of refugees is therefore frequently a coded attack on Muslims, for the words "Muslim," "asylum-seeker," "refugee," and "immigrant" become synonymous and interchangeable in the popular imagination. In this case, the common experiences of immigrant communities of unemployment, rejection, alienation and violence have combined with Islamophobia to make integration particularly difficult.

This has led Muslim communities to suffer higher levels of unemployment, poor housing, poor health and higher levels of racially motivated violence than other communities. For example, in 2003, when the Home Office produced a poster about alleged deceit and dishonesty amongst people seeking asylum, it chose to illustrate its concerns by focusing on someone with a Muslim name. An end-of-year article in the *Sunday Times* magazine on "Inhumanity to Man" focused in four of its five examples on actions by Muslims.

There is a widespread perception that the war on terror is in fact a war on Islam.

A second contextual factor is the skeptical, secular and agnostic outlook with regard to religion that is expressed in the media, perhaps particularly the left-liberal media. The outlook is opposed to all religions, not only to Islam. Commenting on media treatment of the Church of England, the Archbishop of Canterbury remarked that the Church in the eyes of the media is "a kind of soap opera . . . It is both ridiculous and fascinating." Ridiculing religion by the media would appear to be even-handed, but since Muslims have less influence and less access to public platforms, attacks are far more undermining. Debates and disagreements about religion are legitimate in modern society and are, indeed, to be welcomed, but they need to take place on a symmetrical basis.

A third contextual factor is foreign policy in the UK [United Kingdom] and most Western countries, in general, regarding various conflict situations around the world. There is a widespread perception that the war on terror is in fact a war on Islam, and that the UK supports Israel against the Palestinians. In other conflicts too the UK government appears to side with non-Muslims against Muslims and to agree with the view that the terms "Muslim" and "terrorist" are synonymous. These perceptions of UK foreign policy may or may not be accurate. The point is that they help fashion the lens through which events are interpreted—not only by Muslims but by non-Muslims as well. . . .

Open and Closed Views Discourage Better Understanding of Muslims

Race equality organizations and activists over many years have failed to include Islamophobia in their programs and campaigns. For instance, why did the Race Relations Amendment Act fail to refer to anti-Muslim prejudice? In order to begin to answer this question, it is useful to draw a key distinction between closed views of Islam, on the one hand, and open views, on the other. Phobic dread of Islam is the recurring characteristic of closed views. Legitimate disagreement and criticism, as well as appreciation and respect, are aspects of open views.

Closed views typically picture Islam as undifferentiated, static and monolithic, and as intolerant of internal pluralism and deliberation. They are therefore insensitive to significant differences and variations within the world of Islam and, in particular, they are unable to appreciate the existence of tensions and disagreements amongst Muslims. For example, they ignore debates about human rights and freedom in Muslim countries and contexts, about appropriate relationships between Islam and other world faiths, and between Islam and secularism. In short, debates and differences which are taken for granted amongst non-Muslims are neither seen nor heard when they take place within Islam.

Sweeping generalizations are then made about all Muslims, in ways which would not happen in the case of, for example, all Roman Catholics, or all Germans, or all Londoners. Also, it is all too easy to argue from the particular to the general in the case of Muslims—any episode in which an individual Muslim is judged to have behaved badly is used as an illustrative example to condemn all Muslims without exception.

Diversity within Islam, like diversity within other religions, is multi-faceted and multi-dimensional. Some of the differences that tend to be ignored or over-simplified in much Islamophobic discourse pertain to those between Muslims of various countries, such as between the Middle East and South Asia, or Iranians and Arabs. Other examples include the difference between Muslims who are profoundly critical of the human rights records of certain Muslim countries and those who maintain that such criticism is merely a symptom of Islamophobia. Other differences that tend to be overlooked are the ones found between the perceptions and experiences of women and men, or the older and younger generations, particularly in the Muslim communities of Western Europe; or the ones between members of different social classes or the wide range of political movements and parties. Another important difference is that between the diverse interpretations of terminologies, doctrines and injunctions in the Qur'an and Islamic traditions, and between major strands and paths in the twentieth century, such as Sufism and Islamism, or movements known as modernism and revivalism.

Phobic dread of Islam is the recurring characteristic of closed views.

A recurring phrase in the Western media nowadays is "fundamentalism," This is not a helpful term. A brief history of the term recalls that it was coined as self-definition by a strand within Christianity and only much later, almost as a metaphor, to criticize aspects of Islam. It is emphatically not a term which Muslims themselves ever use for purposes of self-definition, and the "fundamentals" in Islam to which it claims to refer are of a different order from those to which it refers in Christianity.

Closed views see a total difference between Islam, on the one hand, and the non-Muslim world, particularly the so-called West, on the other. Islam is the "other," with few or no similarities between itself and other civilizations and cultures, and with few or no shared concepts and moral values. Further, Islam is seen as hermetically sealed off from the rest of the world, with no common roots and no borrowing or mixing in either direction.

The alternative, "open" view sees similarities and shared values, as also incidentally shared problems and weaknesses, and many kinds of interaction. In the open view it is impossible to assert that, for example, Islam is "East" and Europe is "West" (or Judeo-Christian), with no inter-connections or commonalities. On the contrary, the open view stresses that there are close links between the three Abrahamic religions. At the same time it acknowledges that there are significant differences between Islam, Christianity and Judaism, and that each has its own specific outlook on what these differences are, and on how they should be managed.

Claims that Islam is different and "other" often involve stereotypes and views about "us" (non-Muslims) and "them" (Muslims), and the notion that "we" are superior, civilized, reasonable, generous, efficient, sophisticated, enlightened, and non-sexist. "They" are primitive, violent, irrational, scheming, disorganized, and oppressive. An open view rejects such simplistic approaches. It acknowledges that Islam is different in significant respects from other religions and from the West, but does not see it as deficient or as less worthy.

A perception of the inferiority of Islam includes such examples as the belief that Muslim cultures mistreat women; that Muslims co-opt religious observance and beliefs to bolster or justify political and military projects; that they do not distinguish between universal religious tenets, on the one hand, and local cultural mores on the other, and that they are compliant, unreflective and literalist in their interpretation of scriptures.

Closed views see Islam as violent and aggressive, firmly committed to barbaric terrorism, and implacably hostile to the non-Muslim world. Islam was once, said [British journalist] Peregrine Worsthorne in the early 1990s, "a great civilization worthy of being argued with, but now it has degenerated into a primitive enemy fit only to be sensitively subjugated." Thus, Islam is perceived as a threat to global peace:

Muslim fundamentalism is fast becoming the chief threat to global peace and security as well as a cause of national and local disturbance through terrorism. It is akin to the menace posed by Nazism and fascism in the 1930s and then by Communism in the 1950s.

Islam means "submission" (not "peace") and it is the aim of Muslims ("those who have submitted") to make the whole world submit. The teaching seems not to envisage the idea of Muslims as a minority, except as a temporary phenomenon. The best that non-Muslims—in Britain that means Sikhs and Hindus, as well as Jews and Christians—can hope for is that they be treated as "*dhimmis,*" second-class citizens within the Islamic state.

It is frequently alleged that Muslims use their religion for strategic, political and military advantage rather than as a religious faith and as a way of life shaped by a comprehensive legal tradition. The [London] *Observer* article which first popularized the term "Muslim fundamentalism," asserted that Islam had been "revived by the ayatollahs and their admirers as a device, indistinguishable from a weapon, for running a modern state." Muslims are assumed to have an instrumental or manipulative view of their religion rather than to be sincere in their beliefs, for their faith is "indistinguishable from a weapon."

Even organizations and individuals known for their liberalism and anti-racism express prejudice against Islam and Muslims.

Islamophobia in Britain is often mixed with racism—violence and harassment on the streets, and direct or indirect discrimination in the workplace. A closed view of Islam has the effect of justifying such racism. The expression of a closed view in the media, for example, gives support and comfort to racist behavior. Islamophobia merges with crude color racism, since most Muslims are perceived to have black or brown skins, and also anti-immigrant prejudice, since Muslims in Britain are perceived to have alien customs, specifically Asian.

The expression of anti-Muslim ideas and sentiments is getting increasingly acceptable. They are natural, taken-for-granted ingredients of the everyday world of millions of people.

It is not only the tabloid newspapers that demonize Islam. There are routine derogatory references in all the press, in pamphlets and books. Even organizations and individuals known for their liberalism and anti-racism express prejudice against Islam and Muslims. As one correspondent put it: "A deep dislike of Islam is not a new phenomenon in our society. What is new is the way it is articulated today by those sections of society who claim the mantle of secularism, liberalism and tolerance . . . They preach equality of opportunities for all, yet turn a blind eye to the fact that this society offers only unequal opportunities for Muslims."

How Can Islamophobia Be Fought?

To answer this we must examine its cause. Firstly, there is prejudice; unfortunately, education is not enough to dispel it. Secondly, there is the smear of terrorism. The third cause is ignorance of which the *hijab* [Muslim style of dress] issue is a classic example. I wonder how far Muslims realize that non-Muslims have little understanding of Islamic distinctiveness. Only grass-roots contact can combat this. I recently spoke in a mosque at a Christian-Muslim "Meeting for Better Understanding." The priest and I presented the position of our respective religions on a specific topic, and these meetings have proved immensely helpful in building mutual understanding.

Finally, the fourth cause is the lack of democracy in the Muslim world. Here is the one issue where critics of Islam have a point. Most Muslim states are repressive and only a minority are genuine democracies. In addition, far too many non-Muslim minorities there are marginalized if not harassed. Even if the average Briton rarely darkens a chapel door, traditional British sense of fair play will cause him to view negatively the denial of religious liberty and/or equality to non-Muslims, especially to Christians.

Muslims need to rediscover the art of generosity. They should think of Islam as a garden.

It is sad that some of the greatest enemies of Islam can be found in the dictators of Muslim countries. The best solution to the stagnation of the current Muslim *ummah* (global nation) and to Islamophobia itself is to apply true Islamic principles based on the Holy Qur'an and Hadith. According to the great Muslim thinker, Muhammed Qutub, the best way to counteract hostility to Islam and Muslims is through faith. A secular and non-religious approach will not solve the current crisis, but a solution can be found with new and brave ideas, regardless of their source, as long as they follow and adhere to Islamic principles.

Muslims need to rediscover the art of generosity. They should think of Islam as a garden. The thing about a garden is that all this truly monumental variety of life exits in symbiosis: nourishing each other and ensuring the overall survival of the garden. Of course the garden has to be tended: the weeds have to be cleared, plants have to be pruned, and we have to make sure that nothing over-grows—that is, no single interpretation becomes an overarching, totalitarian ideology so much that it ends up suffocating and endangering other plants. It is not for nothing that the garden is the central metaphor of the Islamic paradise.

11

Racial Profiling Against Latinos Must Be Addressed

Anthony E. Mucchetti

Anthony E. Mucchetti is a graduate of Harvard Law School.

The continued migration of Latinos and Hispanics into further interior regions of the United States necessitates a better understanding and awareness on the part of law enforcement personnel. "Driving while brown," a spinoff from the famous "driving while black" accusation of police-instigated racial profiling, has become a common accusation among Hispanics and Latinos living in areas such as the Midwest.

Bonnie Castro's Montana license plate read "PUREMEX" and was intended as an expression of pride in her family heritage. "We didn't think it would make us a target," she later explained after having been detained for almost forty minutes in ninety-degree weather while holding her five-month-old son as police canines searched her car for illegal drugs. The Billings [Montana] Police Department later explained that their actions were justified since Ms. Castro circled the block six times as members of a special police unit were arresting suspected drug dealers nearby. However, given the time that elapsed between when she clocked out of work and when the officer radioed in the call, Ms. Castro would have had to complete a half dozen loops in less than one minute for the police

Anthony E. Mucchetti, "Driving While Brown: A Proposal for Ending Racial Profiling in Emerging Latino Communities," *Harvard Latino Law Review*, Volume 8, Spring 2005. Copyright © 2005 by the President and fellows of Harvard College. Reproduced by permission.

department's explanation to make sense. Following a thorough inspection of her car, which failed to yield contraband, Ms. Castro was issued citations for driving without proof of insurance and having an expired registration. The court dismissed both tickets the following day. Unfortunately, this incident was not Castro's first brush with local law enforcement. Just two weeks earlier, she had been stopped by the Billings Police Department for honking her horn and waving to a neighbor. The officer explained that car horns should be sounded only in an emergency or as a warning. Despite this explanation, Ms. Castro wondered whether she had been the victim of racial profiling, since the local police department rarely issued citations or warnings due to the improper use of a horn.

The criminalization of race takes on special meaning in the context of traffic stops.

License Plates Are a Way to Show Pride, but Invite Profiling

The text of Bonnie Castro's license plate evinced a public choice to celebrate her ethnic roots. For many Latinos, however, the color of their skin alone is an equally visible—and immutable—marker of their ancestry. In this sense, color can serve as the equivalent of a license plate or bumper sticker which labels an individual and subjects him or her to racial and ethnic stereotypes. As [University of Pittsburgh School of Law] Professor David Harris observed:

> Police can use skin color as evidence of criminal involvement, even without any other evidence that points in that direction. This means, in clear and unequivocal terms, that *skin color itself has been criminalized.* This approach to law enforcement stigmatizes every African American, Latino, Asian, or member of any other minority group whose un-

changeable personal characteristics, like black or brown skin, . . . become physical markers of criminality, more indelible than any scarlet letter.

Profiling Invites Commentary

The criminalization of race takes on special meaning in the context of traffic stops. Statistics and studies overwhelmingly support the contention that racial profiling—commonly described as "the detention, interdiction or other disparate treatment of an individual [by police] solely on the basis of the racial or ethnic status of such individual"—has occurred for decades on our nation's streets and highways. This has led commentators to assert that dark skin, by itself, effectively functions as probable cause to stop a vehicle and conduct a search. The notion that many officers pursue race-conscious policing policies has even made it into the popular lexicon in the form of the terms "driving while black" or "driving while brown"—which some facetiously describe as "unwritten violation[s] in the state's traffic code." This phenomenon has been referenced in newspapers, academic journals, and even popular culture. For instance, an animated cartoon series on cable television recently depicted a scene in which a police officer stopped an African American and asked, "Do you know how 'black' you were going?" The puzzled motorist responded, "Somewhere between Denzel Washington and Nelly?"

To cure an affliction, one must first diagnose the disease.

However, racial profiling is no laughing matter. The situations faced by this fictional cartoon character and real victims such as Bonnie Castro are representative of those confronting a growing number of minorities, including many Latinos. Recent figures released by the U.S. Census Bureau indicate that Latinos are rapidly expanding well beyond the Southwest into "non-traditional" areas such as Billings, Montana, and Noel,

Missouri. As a result, bustling cities and rural towns through-out middle America are experiencing Latino "hypergrowth." For instance, the Latino population in Tulsa, Oklahoma, in-creased by 303% between 1980 and 2000; Nashville, Tennes-see, witnessed a growth in the Hispanic population of 630%; and the number of Latinos living in Raleigh, North Carolina, jumped by 1180%. Defying typical notions of where Latinos reside, the largest overall statewide increase in the Hispanic population did not occur in Texas or California, but rather in Arkansas, where there was a net growth of 170% over a ten-year period. These demographic trends are reshaping the tra-ditional image of the Heartland: "The prototypical Midwest-ern farm town—almost all white, English-speaking, of European heritage, and mostly middle class—is becoming di-verse culturally, racially, and class-wise. Virtually overnight, small rural towns gained a significant Latina/o presence."

Latinos Need Better Organization

As Latinos move into communities in the Midwest and South-east, however, they become more vulnerable to discriminatory practices such as racial profiling. Their increased susceptibility is due to a combination of factors: in the Midwest, the Latino population is more diffuse, there are fewer legal advocacy re-sources in rural areas, and little protective legislation is in place which either provides for the collection of data pertain-ing to traffic stops or bans racial profiling altogether. Com-mentator Sylvia Lazos Vargas [of the University of Missouri School of Law] explained that many Latinos would have diffi-culty incorporating themselves into the Midwestern culture due to racial, ethnic, and language differences:

> The influx of Latinas/os is felt immediately and visibly. There is no possibility of Latinas/os remaining "olvidados," or unseen. . . . Spaces in rural America are small and con-tained, neighbors know one another. These are communities

where newcomers are immediately noticed and scrutinized. The sense of who is a newcomer spans generations, not years; counties, not countries.

Further, some studies indicate that racial profiling of Latinos occurs more frequently in "hyper-growth rural communities" in states like Missouri, where police stop Hispanics at rates 12% to 1250% higher than their proportion of the local population.

Concerted Efforts Must Be Made

These factors, in tandem, suggest that individuals in emerging Latino communities will be repeatedly victimized by race-conscious policing until a comprehensive solution is adopted to eradicate such practices. Accordingly, I propose that the government undertake an expansive, sustained, and targeted effort to collect data with regard to the conditions under which federal, state, and local law enforcement officials stop and search individuals. Although certain states and localities collect related information pursuant to consent decrees, voluntary policies, or legislation, often such studies are performed in an incomplete manner. Given that Latinos have settled throughout the country, nothing short of a nationwide data collection effort will determine where racial profiling occurs and pinpoint its underlying causes. This solution is based on a simple premise: to cure an affliction, one must first diagnose the disease. As a result of this nationwide study, federal and state legislators will be provided with the information necessary to form enlightened policies for dealing with racial profiling. This research may also help to build the political will necessary to pass such laws by definitively proving the existence of the phenomenon. As such, my proposal is not a panacea that will, by itself, eliminate race-conscious police practices. Rather, it is a necessary first step that will mark the beginning of the end of racial profiling.

12

Discrimination and Racial Profiling Threaten Democracy

Peter van Onselen

Peter van Onselen is an associate professor in politics and government at Edith Cowan University in Perth, Western Australia. He is a contributing editor at The Australian *and also writes a weekly column in the* News Limited *Sunday papers.*

Once considered bastions of democracy, countries such as Australia and the United States are gradually sliding into a gray area in which bigotry, particularly against Muslims, is masked under the pretense of security. There is no such thing as politically correct bias; bigotry—however justifiable it may seem—threatens to override the very foundations of freedom and democracy upon which nations such as these were built.

Fostering the notion of "the other'" is the sort of divisive thinking that should be corrected in individuals early in life, for a cornerstone of democracy is that everyone is treated equally before the law.

In practice, of course, variables such as wealth can skew such a principle, but that doesn't mean we shouldn't continue to work towards creating the kind of harmony between religions or racial groupings that helps make our liberal democracy function more effectively.

Since the September 11, 2001 terrorist attacks on the World Trade Center and the Pentagon there has been a raft of examples of unnecessary discrimination against people of Middle Eastern descent or appearance, the misguided assumption being that they are more likely to be terrorists.

It is a form of racial profiling.

This week [January 2009], yet another instance came to public attention. An airline passenger in the US was awarded nearly $350,000 in compensation for being forced to cover up the T-shirt with Arabic script on it that he was wearing when trying to board a flight in August 2006, nearly five years after the 9/11 attacks. He was told wearing such a shirt at an airport was the equivalent of "wearing a T-shirt at a bank stating, 'I am a robber.'" Not much tolerance there.

At least the court sent the right message.

There has been a raft of examples of unnecessary discrimination against people of Middle Eastern descent or appearance.

Profiling Is Unfair and Adds to Problems

More disturbingly, and closer to home [Australia] Boeing won a landmark decision this week before the Queensland [Australia] Anti-Discrimination Tribunal allowing it to refuse to employ people born in countries, mostly in the Middle East, that are proscribed as terrorist by the US, when working on US military aircraft. US security regulations prevent people born in such countries from working on defence projects so Boeing needed the ruling to enable it to continue its operations in Queensland.

Rather than collectively refuse to comply with the regulations, aerospace companies such as Boeing have sought exemptions from anti-discrimination legislation all over the world to enable them to secure lucrative military contracts.

It shouldn't be all that surprising that the US is happy to apply such discrimination on the basis of where people are born. You cannot become US president unless you are born a US citizen. Supporters of [Austrian-born California Governor] Arnold Schwarzenegger have been trying for years to get that part of the Constitution changed.

Racial profiling is a highly contentious and discriminatory approach to law enforcement. It targets people of certain racial appearances, not for anything suspicious they might have done, but simply because of the colour of their skin.

Its advocates claim that as with any other form of profiling it is a useful tool that shouldn't be discounted out of hand. Opponents, such as Amnesty International, argue that racial profiling makes Muslim communities less prepared to assist in the so-called war on terror. Most academic literature shows that racial profiling causes more harm than good when it is put into practice.

Racial profiling is a highly contentious and discriminatory approach to law enforcement.

Vigilance, or Bigotry?

Shortly after the Mumbai India terrorist incident in late November last year [2008], former Howard [former Australian Prime Minister John Howard] government minister for justice and customs, now Opposition spokesman for defence, Senator David Johnston, told a journalist "educated bigotry" was a useful method for targeting suspected terrorists at Australian airports.

His comments generated surprisingly little interest, given their explosive nature. Johnston was referring to what he described as a "commonsense" approach whereby law enforcement personnel should target people with Middle Eastern names and appearances.

"When you've got a random choice of, say, several hundred people coming through an airport at one time and you've got no other intelligence, other than how people look, it distils down basically to bigotry," Johnston told *News Limited* journalist Paul Lampathakis.

He had made similar remarks at a Chatham House rules lunch in Perth [Australia's capital city] I had attended two weeks earlier. His remarks, however startling, would ordinarily have remained off the record. However, when he was approached by Lampathakis, also an attendee at the lunch, to put his views on the public record, Johnston happily obliged.

'Educated bigotry is a contradiction in terms.'

Australian Customs Service personnel do not officially engage in the practice of racial profiling. However, given that Johnston previously had portfolio responsibilities in that area, you have to wonder what the unofficial policy entails.

Democracy Cannot Thrive amid Bigotry

Labor's Minister for Home Affairs, Bob Debus, is in no doubt how Johnston's analysis should be viewed.

Debus told me "educated bigotry is a contradiction in terms. It reminds me of crazy phrenologists in the 19th century who thought you could tell a criminal by the shape of their skull. The entire argument is unacceptable."

Johnston went further in his defence of educated bigotry, making a rather bizarre link in logic to the World War II internment of German and Japanese people. He said Australia did so "for good reason".

Never mind that governments the world over have apologised for their World War II internment policies.

The practice was one of the most shameful acts by the Allies in the war. US president Ronald Reagan signed legislation in 1988 that stated that internment policies were based on "race prejudice, war hysteria, and a failure of political leadership".

Political leaders play an important role in the shaping of public opinion. They need to lead by example.

In 1988, when [former Prime Minister] John Howard advocated a reduction in Asian immigration to preserve cultural harmony in Australia, he was rightly condemned, including by [Australian House of Representatives member] Philip Ruddock.

Years later Howard himself admitted he was wrong.

The world is at present distracted by the pressing concerns of the global financial crisis. Fair enough. But Western nations in particular need to ensure they treat people from different ethnic backgrounds equally and fairly. That's what liberal democracy is all about.

Recent examples at home and abroad suggest we are falling short of the mark.

Organizations to Contact

The editors have compiled the following list of organizations concerned with the issues debated in this book. The descriptions are derived from materials provided by the organizations. All have publications or information available for interested readers. The list was compiled on the date of publication of the present volume; the information provided here may change. Readers need to remember that many organizations take several weeks or longer to respond to inquiries.

American Civil Liberties Union (ACLU)
125 Broad St., 18th Floor, New York, NY   10004
Web site: www.aclu.org

The best-known and longest-standing organization for civil rights and liberties in the United States, the ACLU takes a proactive role in protecting citizens against racial, ethnic, and religious profiling. Recent ACLU activities have involved racial justice, gay rights, and personal-freedom issues involving national security. The organization offers publications and articles on its Web site.

Amnesty International USA
5 Penn Plaza, New York, NY   10001
(212) 807-8400 • fax: (212) 627-1451
Web site: www.amnestyusa.org

Amnesty International is a worldwide organization that champions human rights and intercedes in all types of rights-related cases, including those of alleged racial profiling. Recent cases within the international realm include stopping forced evictions in Rome, Italy; in the United States, civil liberties versus airport security remains an important issue. Current and back-issue publications and newsletters can be found on the organization's Web site.

Asian-Nation

Web site: www.asiannation.org

A Web site geared toward Asian-Americans, Asian-Nation welcomes articles about and provides information regarding challenges, including racial profiling, that concern Americans of Asian descent. The Web site offers a discussion opportunity for all issues relating to Asian-Americans, and its articles have been reproduced in such periodicals as the *Washington Post* and *USA Today*, as well as online at PBS.org and AmericanGov.org.

League of United Latin American Citizens (LULAC)

2000 L St. NW, Washington, DC   20036
(202) 833-6130 • fax: (202) 833-6135
Web site: www.lulac.org

The largest Latino advocacy organization in the United States, LULAC strives for equal opportunity and justice for all citizens of Latino/Hispanic heritage. Current issues of concern include the areas of racial profiling against and assimilation of Latinos in interior-U.S. areas where such populations are beginning to grow. *LULAC News*, the organization's monthly publication, can be accessed on its Web site and hard copies are available to subscribers.

Muslim American Society (MAS)

PO Box 1896, Falls Church, VA   22041
(703) 998-6525 • fax: (703) 998-6526
Web site: www.masnet.org

The Muslim American Society is a charitable, religious, social, cultural, and educational nonprofit organization. It is a pioneering Islamic organization, an Islamic revival, and reform movement that uplifts the individual, family, and society and seeks to improve relations among Muslims and non-Muslims in the United States. Current issues involve the problem of racial profiling and overall mistrust of Muslims within the United States. The society's monthly magazine can be obtained through subscription.

National Association for the Advancement of Colored People (NAACP)

NAACP National Headquarters, Baltimore, MD   21215
(410) 580-5777
Web site: www.naacp.org

Founded in 1909, the mission of the NAACP is to ensure the political, educational, social, and economic equality of rights of all persons and to eliminate racial hatred and racial discrimination. Recently, the NAACP joined forces with other groups (such as LULAC) representing minorities in an effort to combat racial profiling. The leading publication of the NAACP is *The Advocate*, to which one may subscribe or research back issues on the organization's Web site.

National Association of Police Organizations (NAPO)

317 S Patrick St., Alexandria, Virginia   22314
(703) 549-0775 • fax: (703) 684-0515
e-mail: info@napo.org
Web site: www.napo.org

The National Association of Police Organizations is a coalition of police unions and associations from across the United States that serves to advance the interests of America's law enforcement officers. Along with a huge constituency of current and retired officers, NAPO's membership includes more than 100,000 citizens who share with the police a common dedication to fair and effective crime control and law enforcement. The organization offers information, news, and press releases on its Web site.

Bibliography

Books

Geoffrey P. Alpert, Roger G. Dunham, and Meghan S. Stroshine	*Policing: Continuity and Change.* Long Grove, IL: Waveland Press, Inc., 2006.
William Ayers, Rick Ayers, Bernardine Dohrn, et al.	*Zero Tolerance: Resisting the Drive for Punishment in Our Schools.* New York: New Press, 2001.
Cynthia Brown, ed.	*Lost Liberties: Ashcroft and the Assault on Personal Liberties.* New York: New Press, 2003.
Alejandro del Carmen	*Racial Profiling in America.* Upper Saddle River, NJ: Pearson Prentice Hall, 2008.
Robert F. Drinan	*The Mobilization of Shame: A World View of Human Rights.* New Haven, CT: Yale University Press, 2001.
Darin D. Fredrickson	*Racial Profiling: Eliminating the Confusion Between Racial and Criminal Profiling and Clarifying What Constitutes Unfair Discrimination and Persecution.* Springfield, IL: Charles C. Thomas, 2002.

Karen S. Glover   *Racial Profiling: Research, Racism and Resistance*. Lanham, MD: Rowman and Littlefield, 2009.

David A. Harris   *Profiles in Injustice: Why Racial Profiling Cannot Work*. New York: New Press, 2001.

Thomas J. Hickey, ed.   *Taking Sides: Clashing Views in Crime and Criminology*, 9th ed. New York: McGraw-Hill Companies, Inc., 2010.

Kenneth Meeks   *Driving While Black*. New York: Broadway Books, 2000.

Mia Nodeen Moody   *Black and Mainstream Press' Framing of Racial Profiling: A Historical Perspective*. Lanham, MD: University Press of America, 2008.

Steven Muffler, ed.   *Racial Profiling: Issues, Data and Analysis*. New York: Nova Press, 2006.

Joycelyn M. Pollock   *Ethical Dilemmas and Decisions in Criminal Justice*, 6th ed. Belmont, CA: Wadsworth, Cengage Learning, 2010.

Frank Schmallenger and John Worrall   *Policing Today*. Upper Saddle River, NJ: Pearson Education, Inc., 2010.

Randall G. Shelden, Sharon K. Tracy, and William B. Brown   *Youth Gangs in American Society*, 3rd ed. Belmont, CA: Wadsworth, Thomson Learning, Inc., 2004.

Ronald Weitzer and Steven A. Tuch — *Race and Policing in America: Conflict and Reform*. New York: Cambridge University Press, 2006.

Terry White — *Blacks and Whites in America: Eighteen Essays on Race*. Jefferson, NC: McFarland & Company, 2003.

Periodicals

Cyril Josh Barker — "New TSA Regulations Bellow Racial Profiling," *New York Amsterdam News*, January 7, 2010.

Boston College Third World Law Journal — "Racial Profiling in the Name of National Security: Protecting Minority Travelers' Civil Liberties in an Age of Terrorism," Winter 2010.

Richard Carter — "Gates-Gate Will Linger Due to Obama's 'Stupid' Comment," *New York Amsterdam News*, August 6, 2009.

Shaun L. Gabbidon, et al. — "The Influence of Race/Ethnicity on the Perceived Prevalence and Support for Racial Profiling at Airports," *Criminal Justice Policy Review*, September 2009.

Cynthia Gordy — "And Justice For All," *Essence*, September 2009.

Lisa Graziano, et al. — "Police Misconduct, Media Coverage and Public Perception of Racial Profiling: An Experiment," *Justice Quarterly*, February 2010.

Mehdi Hasan   "Spooked By the Underwear Bomber," *New Statesman*, January 11, 2010.

George Higgins, et al.   "Exploring the Influence of Race Relations and Public Safety Concerns on Public Support for Racial Profiling During Traffic Stops," *International Journal of Police Science & Management*, Spring 2010.

Stephon Johnson   "Hikind Pushes for Racial/Religious Profiling Bill Again," *New York Amsterdam News*, December 31, 2009.

Richard J. Lundman   "Are Police-reported Driving While Black Data a Valid Indicator of the Race and Ethnicity of the Traffic Law Violators Police Stop? A Negative Answer with Minor Qualifications," *Journal of Criminal Justice*, January 2010.

Jack McDevitt   "Political Influences on Racial Disparities in Traffic Enforcement Policies," *Criminology & Public Policy*, May 2009.

Kirk Miller   "Race, Driving, and Police Organization: Modeling Moving and Nonmoving Traffic Stops with Citizen Self-Reports of Driving Practices," *Journal of Criminal Justice*, November 2009.

Lekan Oguntoyinbo   "Taking A Stand," *Diverse: Issues in Higher Education*, February 4, 2010.

Sunghoon Roh, et al.   "A Geographic Approach to Racial Profiling: The Microanalysis and Macroanalysis of Racial Disparity in Traffic Stops," *Police Quarterly*, June 2009.

Vic Satzewich and William Saffir   "Racism versus Professionalism: Claims and Counterclaims About Racial Profiling," *Canadian Journal of Criminology and Criminal Justice*, April 2009.

Deborah J. Schildkraut   "The Dynamics of Public Opinion on Racial Profiling After 9/11: Results from a Survey Experiment," *American Behavioral Scientist*, September 2009.

Eric A. Stewart, et al.   "Neighborhood Racial Context and Perceptions of Police-Based Racial Discrimination Among Black Youth," *Criminology*, August 2009.

Index